CHINA

Recipes, Flavors & Traditions

P.J. Tierney

KITCHEN INK

KITCHEN INK's passionate Kids in the Kitchen team of recipe creators, testers, editors, food stylists, photographers, and designers work tirelessly to create products that introduce kids to cooking. Having fun, making memories in the kitchen, and creating a delicious meal is what we are all about.

Our easy-to-follow, creative, and delicious recipes—kid-tested and parent-approved—include both healthy meals and special treats. Adult supervision and safety first are always important in the kitchen. We hope you enjoy our books as much as we have loved creating them.

Download a free culinary passport pdf. This passport has all pages; it does not contain the stickers found in the culinary passport sold with *The Global Cookbook, Delicious Recipes from Seven Continents*.
ISBN: 978-1-943016-22-8
www.kitcheninkpublishing.com

Copyright © 2025 by Kitchen Ink Publishing

Recipes, text, and photographs by Kitchen Ink Publishing.

Publisher's Note
While every care has been taken in compiling the recipes for this book, neither Kitchen Ink Publishing, nor any other persons who have worked on this publication, can accept responsibility for any errors or omissions, inadvertent or not, that may be found in the recipes or text, nor for any problems that may arise as a result of preparing these recipes. If you have any special dietary requirements, restrictions, or medical conditions, it is advisable to consult a medical professional before following any of the recipes contained in this book.

All rights reserved. No part of this publication may be reproduced, distributed, or transmitted in any form or by any means, including photocopying, recording, or other electronic or mechanical methods, without the prior written permission of the publisher, except in the case of brief quotations embodied in critical articles and reviews. For information, write to Kitchen Ink Subsidiary Rights Department, 114 John Street, #277, New York, NY 10038.

Library of Congress Cataloging-in-Publication data is available.
ISBN 978-1-943016-31-0

First Edition
28 29 27 26 25   10 9 8 7 6 5 4 3 2 1

Printed in China

Kitchen Ink Publishing
114 John Street, #277
New York, NY 10038

Kitchen Ink books may be purchased for educational, business, or sales promotional use. For information, please email the Special Markets Department at sales@kitcheninkpublishing.com.

See what Kitchen Ink is up to, share recipes and tips, and shop our store—www.kitcheninkpublishing.com.

  kitcheninkpublishing

Jeanne,

my sister and fellow world traveler. Our adventures on the Great Wall, lunch in Shenzhen with fish in my pockets, and time spent with you are treasured memories.

Introduction by P.J. Tierney

CHINA, People's Republic of China. The architecture, the history, traditions... and, oh, the food. I was fortunate to be able to visit China, Thailand, and Bali with my sister Jeanne. We started our trip in Hong Kong, where some friends who lived there shared some Chinese customs and traditions with us.

In large cities in China, many families live in apartments, often with grandparents. Families respect hierarchy and honor traditions, like cooking and eating together, usually three meals a day with some snacks in between. Superstition and tradition dictate that certain foods must be consumed for specific festivals/events to invoke a blessing.

The Chinese don't eat with knives and forks but with chopsticks. As chopsticks don't chop, all food is very soft or cut into bite-size pieces before cooking. According to Chinese custom, you should place your chopsticks across the top of your rice bowl or on the chopstick holder when finished eating; do not stick them in your food or leave them misplaced around the table. Interesting fact: China uses 45 billion pairs of chopsticks a year. I recommend you secure your own chopsticks and practice using them while eating the delicious food you make. It will take some practice, but with time, you will become a whiz and show your friends how to use chopsticks properly.

I learned not to finish all my food. In Chinese culture, leaving a small amount of food uneaten is a sign of appreciation; it shows that your host or the restaurant provided enough food to make you full and content.

To provide you with a taste of what is eaten in China, I've included recipes for breakfast, small plates, sides & snacks, entrées, and desserts and welcome you to try them all.

Traditional Chinese breakfast recipes include Donut Sticks on page 7 and Congee/Rice Porridge on page 14. Ji Dan Bing is an egg wrapped in a pancake prepared and served at many Chinese street carts, perfect for a grab-and-go breakfast; recipe on page 12. Noodles are eaten even for breakfast, and on page 48, there is an easy recipe for homemade noodles for any time of the day.

Tea is more than just a drink in China, encompassing centuries-old traditions; it represents harmony, respect, and hospitality. The art of brewing and drinking tea is considered an important social ritual, and tea houses are popular gathering spots for friends and families. Boba/Bubble Tea originated in Taiwan in the 1980s; I've included this delicious beverage on page 4 as you will enjoy making it as much as drinking it.

The phrase *dim sum* comes from the Cantonese *tim sam,* meaning "appetizer". You can make Steamed Vegetable Dumplings on page 37, Traditional Pork Fried Rice on page 25, or try Spring Rolls on page 30, and on page 20, my favorite Lettuce Wraps.

For lunch, the menu is usually simple: Tomato and Egg Noodle Soup, page 40; Sesame Noodles eaten hot or cold, page 64, and on page 52, Sweet and Sour Chicken, to name a few.

Dinner is the most important meal, often shared with family. Steamed white rice is usually prepared in a rice cooker and placed in small bowls; dishes of flavorful Chicken Stir Fry, page 46, Beef Lo Mein, page 54, Vegetable Stir Fry, page 58, and others are placed in the middle of the table and each person adds a little of each dish to their rice bowl.

You might think that Chinese desserts are less colorful than their Italian and Mexican counterparts, BUT the flavor packs a punch. I do love chocolate, and the soymilk chocolate pudding on page 76 is smooth and tasty. Top with whipped cream and chocolate shavings, and it not only tastes good, but it is also one good-looking dessert! I was puzzled when I first heard of fried ice cream – how can something frozen be fried? Turn to page 80 to learn how to make this delicious treat, and top with the salted butterscotch sauce on page 82, so YUMMY! The traditional Hong Kong Egg Tarts on page 83 are perfect for a crowd, and you can purchase premade egg tart crusts or make your own from scratch on page 85.

I love a great party theme, and if you throw a Chinese New Year party, learn about the traditions on page 89 and have fun creating personalized fortunes and inserting them into the fortune cookies you are baking, page 68.

Seeing the Great Wall of China, a Wonder of the World, was number one on our to-do list, and to our amazement, the morning we went, there were very few tourists. We hiked the wall, marveling at the views. At one point, we were the only two people on a section of the wall. We climbed stairs and took photos, and my sister and I even danced on the Great Wall of China. I sat on the steps and wrote in my journal—one of my fondest memories. Read more about the Wall on page 87.

This book is part of the Culinary Passport Series; when you complete the Egg Foo Young recipe on page 2, the Crab Rangoon recipe on page 33, and Nian Gao on page 74, place the corresponding sticker in your culinary passport or mark the recipe to track your success and journey around the world through food.

Thanks for joining me on this culinary adventure. Enjoy!

P.J. Tierney

A Note from the Kids in the Kitchen Team

Each recipe notes the number of servings and the time needed to prepare the dish. Please note, the recommended chilling time for a dish may not be included in its active preparation time.

This cookbook includes easy recipes and those requiring a little more patience and skill. As you become more comfortable preparing recipes, it is important to be challenged and improve your kitchen skills.

An adult should be with you to assist, especially when using a knife and the stovetop, and when putting your delicious dishes into and bringing them out of the hot oven. It is up to the adult to decide when you can be more independent in the kitchen.

Step-by-step directions tell you what you need to prepare the dish. Read each recipe completely before you begin and make sure you have all the tools and ingredients you need. These recipes are written for kids all around the globe and both US measurements and metrics are included.

Sometimes a recipe may call for an ingredient you do not have. A substitution will be offered for an international ingredient that may be challenging to find. Please note that if an ingredient is marked "optional," you can leave it out of the recipe if you choose.

If you are vegetarian, you will find recipes without meat or with suggestions to prepare meatless versions of the dish.

Everyone is excited to taste the food they have created BUT, hit the brakes. Food is piping hot when removed from the oven. Always be patient and let the food cool before sampling. Your tongue will thank you.

Always clean up the kitchen when you are done and remember that more hands make light work. Have a cleanup party and everyone is rewarded with dessert.

Contents

Breakfast

Egg Foo Young...2
Boba Tea (Bubble Tea)...4
Donut Sticks..7
Tomato Egg Stir-Fry..10
Ji Dan Bing (Chinese Breakfast Pancake) 12
Congee (Rice Porridge)...14
Tea Eggs...16

Small Plates, Sides & Snacks

Lettuce Wraps 20
Egg Rolls..22
Coleslaw...24
Pork Fried Rice 25
Egg Drop Soup 28
Spring Rolls...30
Crab Rangoon 33
Wonton Wrappers..36
Steamed Vegetable Dumplings 37
Tomato and Egg Noodle Soup 40
Broccoli with Garlic Sauce..42

Entrées

Chicken Stir Fry 46
Easy Homemade Noodles...48
Birthday Noodles with Peanut Sauce 50

Sweet and Sour Chicken 52
Beef Lo Mein 54
Sesame Chicken 56
Vegetable Stir Fry.. 58
Chicken Chow Mein 60
Sweet and Sour Spareribs... 62
Sesame Noodles.. 64

Desserts

Fortune Cookies 68
Snowflake Cake 71
Nian Gao (Lunar New Year Cake).. 74
Chocolate Soymilk Pudding 76
Almond Cookies 78
Fried Ice Cream 80
Salted Butterscotch Sauce 82
Hong Kong Egg Tarts 83
Butter Pastry Tart Crust 85

The Great Wall of China.. 87
Chinese New Year 89

Breakfast

Egg Foo Young...2
Boba Tea (Bubble Tea)...4
Donut Sticks..7
Tomato Egg Stir-Fry..10
Ji Dan Bing (Chinese Breakfast Pancake) 12
Congee (Rice Porridge)...14
Tea Eggs...16

Egg Foo Young

 20 minutes   6 servings

Culinary Passport Recipe

Ingredients

8 large eggs, lightly beaten

½ red bell pepper, finely chopped

1 stalk celery, sliced thin

½ cup (120 milliliters) mushrooms, finely chopped

½ onion, finely chopped

½ cup (120 milliliters) fresh bean sprouts, chopped

4 green onions, chopped green & white parts

½ teaspoon (2.5 milliliters) kosher salt

¼ teaspoon (1.2 milliliters) white pepper

1 cup (240 milliliters) cooked chicken, diced

3 tablespoons (45 milliliters) canola oil

1 ¼ cups (300 milliliters) chicken broth

3 tablespoons (45 milliliters) soy sauce

1 tablespoon (15 milliliters) rice vinegar

2 teaspoons (10 milliliters) brown sugar

1 teaspoon (5 milliliters) sesame oil

2 tablespoons (30 milliliters) cornstarch

3 tablespoons (45 milliliters) cold water

Directions

1. In a large bowl, add the eggs, red pepper, celery, mushrooms, onions, bean sprouts, half the green onions, salt, white pepper, and chicken.

2. In a small saucepan, combine chicken broth, soy sauce, rice vinegar, brown sugar, and sesame oil over low heat.

3. In a small bowl, blend cornstarch and water. Slowly whisk the cornstarch slurry into the saucepan. Continue stirring until the sauce thickens and bubbles.

4. Heat a nonstick skillet with ½ tablespoon (7.5 milliliters) of canola oil over medium heat. Add approximately ½ cup (120 milliliters) of the egg mixture and cook until lightly browned on the bottom. Flip and brown the other side. Plate and keep warm. Repeat until all the batter is gone.

5. Serve warm, topped with the sauce and sprinkled with the rest of the green onions.

Boba Tea (Bubble Tea)

 20 minutes   2 servings

Ingredients

¼ cup (60 milliliters) brown sugar

2 tablespoons (30 milliliters) hot water

½ cup (120 milliliters) instant black tapioca pearls

6 black tea bags or 4 tablespoons (60 milliliters) of loose-leaf black tea

2 cups (480 milliliters) plant-based milk

Ice cubes for a cold drink, optional

Directions

1. In a small bowl, combine the brown sugar and hot water. Stir until the sugar dissolves. If it does not, heat the bowl in the microwave for 1 to 2 minutes, then stir again to form the syrup.
2. Bring a small pot of water to a boil. Cook the tapioca pearls according to the package instructions. Drain and run them under cold tap water for a few seconds to stop cooking. Drain again and transfer them to the bowl of syrup. Let them marinate while preparing the bubble tea.

TIP
Instant Tapioca Pearls take less time to prepare. Bubble tea can be prepared in many ways, using different types of tea or even fruit juice. The original bubble tea always uses black tea.

Breakfast

3. Add 1 cup (240 milliliters) of boiling water and the tea to a glass or pot that's easy to pour from. Let the tea steep for 10 minutes to make it strong. Strain the tea with a fine colander or coffee filter (or remove the tea bags).

4. Add 2 to 3 tablespoons (30 to 45 milliliters) of tapioca pearls and brown sugar syrup to each serving glass. Pour in ½ cup (120 milliliters) of black tea. Add up to 1 cup (240 milliliters) of plant milk, or according to your taste.

5. Stir to mix before drinking. Add more tapioca pearls, syrup, tea, or plant milk to adjust the taste.

6. Serve the drink hot, at room temperature, or add ice cubes to serve it cold.

Donut Sticks

 2 hours 35 minutes   10 sticks

Ingredients

1 ⅔ cups (390 milliliters) all-purpose flour
2 teaspoons (10 milliliters) baking powder
2 large eggs, lightly beaten
½ teaspoon (2.5 milliliters) salt
2 tablespoons (30 milliliters) canola oil
Flour for dusting
Oil for deep frying

Directions

1. In a medium bowl, combine flour, baking powder, eggs, salt, and oil. Mix and knead to make a rough-looking dough. Cover with a damp towel and let it rest for 15 minutes.
2. Apply oil to your clean hands (to prevent sticking), and using your fingers, gently press down and knead the dough until it becomes soft and smooth.

TIP
If you do not have a kitchen thermometer, cut a small piece of dough and carefully place it in the heated oil. The oil is ready if the dough reaches the surface quickly.

Breakfast

3. Roll the dough into a large ball and cut it into two equal-sized balls. Wrap each in plastic wrap and set aside to rest for at least two hours at room temperature.

4. Heat oil in a wok or deep pot for frying.

5. While oil is heating, dust a flat work surface with flour, unwrap a room-temperature dough ball, and use your clean hands to flatten each piece into a rectangle about 4 x 10 inches (10 x 25 cm).

6. Dust the dough lightly with flour to prevent sticking. Then, cut each piece into 5 equal strips. Repeat with the second ball of dough.

7. Once the oil reaches 374°F (190°C), reduce the heat. Gently stretch the dough pieces, then carefully, using tongs, lower two pieces into the oil (be careful not to splash).

8. Roll the dough around continuously with tongs, and when it reaches the surface, stops expanding, and is evenly golden, transfer it to a plate lined with paper towels (to soak up excess oil).

9. Repeat the procedure to cook the rest of the dough. You may cook two sticks simultaneously, but any more will decrease the oil temperature too much, and the dough will not cook properly.

Breakfast

Tomato Egg Stir-Fry

 15 minutes   2 servings

Ingredients

5 eggs

½ teaspoon (2.5 milliliters) salt

¼ teaspoon (1.2 milliliters) pepper

1 teaspoon (5 milliliters) cornstarch

2 tablespoons (30 milliliters) water

2 tablespoons (30 milliliters) vegetable oil

2 stalks green onion, chopped, separating white from green (save green for garnish)

2 tomatoes, stems removed and chopped

3 tablespoons (45 milliliters) ketchup

2 teaspoons (10 milliliters) sugar

¼ cup (60 milliliters) water

Cilantro, chopped for garnish

Directions

1. In a small bowl, crack 5 eggs, season with salt and pepper, and whisk thoroughly to blend.
2. In a small bowl, mix cornstarch with water and set aside.
3. Add vegetable oil to a skillet or wok over medium-high heat. Add the white portion of the green onion. When the onion begins to sizzle, add the tomato and stir-fry for about 1 minute. Then, add the ketchup, sugar, and water; and bring to a boil.
4. Stir in the starch mixture and stir to combine. Remove from heat and pour the mixture into a bowl.
5. Over medium heat, add oil to a clean skillet or wok and add eggs. After ten seconds, when the edges of the eggs begin to set, add the tomato mixture.
6. Gently fold the eggs in half over the tomato and gently break up the large egg pieces with a spatula into the tomato mixture. Stir-Fry everything for 15 to 20 seconds, then turn off the heat.
7. Transfer to a plate and garnish with green onion and cilantro if you like.

Ji Dan Bing (Chinese Breakfast Pancake)

 20 minutes   6 servings

Ingredients

1 tablespoon (15 milliliters) canola oil

1 cup (240 milliliters) all-purpose flour

½ teaspoon (2.5 milliliters) salt

1 cup and 1 tablespoon (255 milliliters) water

3 green onions, sliced

1 tablespoon (15 milliliters) peanut oil (or melted butter)

4 eggs

Toasted black sesame seeds for garnish

Sweet bean sauce (or hoisin sauce)

Chil sauce, optional for spice

2 slices of ham or bacon

Directions

1. Add oil to a medium-sized or small nonstick skillet. Wipe the pan with paper towels to coat evenly with oil. Heat over medium heat until just hot but not smoking.

2. In a medium bowl, add flour, salt, and water, and mix until combined.

3. Add about ⅓ cup (80 milliliters) of the batter to the pan. Immediately swirl the pan so the batter spreads evenly into a thin, round pancake.

4. When the pancake is just set, crack an egg into the center of it. Use a spoon to break the egg and spread it over the pancake. When the egg is still runny, sprinkle it with green onion and black sesame seeds. Cook over medium-low heat until the egg is mostly set and the bottom of the pancake turns golden on the edges. Carefully flip the pancake. Cook for 20 to 30 seconds until the egg is fully cooked. Transfer the pancake to a plate. Keep cooking the rest of the pancakes.

5. Brush the pancake with a thin layer of sweet bean sauce (or hoisin sauce).

Congee (Rice Porridge)

 5 minutes   4 servings

Ingredients

¾ cup (175 milliliters) long-grain rice

9 cups (2,160 milliliters) water (or substitute with a stock of your choice)

1 teaspoon (5 milliliters) salt

Optional: Mix in crushed peanuts, fried egg, and/or chopped scallions

Directions

1. In a large pot, bring the water and rice to a boil.
2. Once boiling, turn the heat down to medium-low and cover with a tilted lid to allow the steam to escape.
3. Cook on medium-low to low heat, stirring until the rice is thick and creamy; about 1 hour.
4. Add salt and optional ingredients to taste.

Tea Eggs

 12 hours and 15 minutes   8 servings

Ingredients

8 eggs at room temperature

2 cups (240 milliliters) water

2 bags of black tea or 1 tablespoon (15 milliliters) of loose tea

1 star anise

1 bay leaf

1 piece of cassia cinnamon (Chinese cinnamon)

½ teaspoon (2.5 milliliters) Sichuan peppercorns or black peppercorns

2 tablespoons (30 milliliters) dark soy sauce

1 tablespoon (15 milliliters) light soy sauce

½ tablespoon (7.5 milliliters) sugar

2 teaspoons (10 milliliters) salt

Directions

1. Fill a large pot with water and bring it to a full boil. Add the eggs, covering them entirely with water. Cover and boil uncovered over medium heat for 8 minutes.

2. While waiting for the eggs to cook, add 2 cups (480 milliliters) of water to a medium saucepan. Add tea, star anise, bay leaf, Chinese cinnamon, Sichuan peppercorns, dark soy sauce, light soy sauce, sugar, and salt. Bring to a boil, then simmer for 3 minutes. Set aside.

3. When the eggs are cooked, transfer them to a large bowl of cold water. Once they're cool enough to touch, gently crack them one by one against the kitchen counter, ensuring the shells are cracked all around.

4. Place the eggs in a container (ideally, one that can fit them snuggly). Pour in the marinade. Cover with a lid and leave to steep for 12 to 24 hours before serving.

Small Plates, Sides & Snacks

Lettuce Wraps 20
Egg Rolls 22
Coleslaw 24
Pork Fried Rice 25
Egg Drop Soup 28
Spring Rolls 30
Crab Rangoon 33
Wonton Wrappers 36
Steamed Vegetable Dumplings 37
Tomato and Egg Noodle Soup 40
Broccoli with Garlic Sauce 42

Lettuce Wraps

 15 minutes　　 20 wraps

Ingredients

1 tablespoon (15 milliliters) neutral cooking oil

1 tablespoon (15 milliliters) minced garlic

1 teaspoon (5 milliliters) minced ginger

1 tablespoon (15 milliliters) Sichuan chili bean paste

1 cup (240 milliliters) minced pork/chicken or crumbled firm tofu

½ cup (120 milliliters) dried shiitake mushroom - rehydrated and finely diced

¾ cups (175 milliliters) celery, finely diced

1 stalk scallions, finely chopped

Fresh chili

Directions

1. Heat oil in a skillet or wok. Stir in garlic, ginger, and Sichuan chili bean paste. Simmer for 10 seconds.
2. Add minced pork, chicken, or tofu. Use a spatula to loosen the mixture and fry until the meat loses its pinkness.
3. Add mushroom and celery. Stir-Fry until they're cooked, but the celery remains crunchy.
4. Add scallions and chili. Stir everything quickly, then transfer to a serving bowl or plate.
5. Fill each lettuce leaf with the stir-fry filling, then serve.

Small Plates, Sides & Snacks

Egg Rolls

 35 minutes   12 servings

Ingredients

1 pound (454 grams) ground pork

1 teaspoon (5 milliliters) ground ginger

1 teaspoon (5 milliliters) garlic powder

1 quart (0.9 liters) vegetable oil for frying

1 tablespoon (15 milliliters) all-purpose flour

1 tablespoon (15 milliliters) water

3 cups (720 milliliters) coleslaw mix or see recipe on page 24

12 egg roll wrappers

Directions

1. In a medium skillet over medium heat, cook the pork, breaking it up as it cooks. When it is halfway cooked, sprinkle the ground ginger and garlic powder on top of the pork and stir to coat the meat evenly. Continue to cook until the pork is no longer pink. Set aside.

2. In another large, heavy pot, heat oil to 375°F (190°C) over medium-high heat. While the oil is heating, combine the flour and water in a bowl until they form a paste. In a separate bowl, combine the coleslaw mix and reserved pork mixture.

3. Lay out one egg roll skin with a corner pointed toward you. Place about ¼ to ⅓ cups (60 to 80 milliliters) of the pork mixture on the egg roll paper, folding the corner up over the mixture. Fold the left and right corners toward the center and continue rolling. Brush some of the flour paste on the final corner to help seal the egg roll.

4. Place the egg rolls into the heated oil and fry, turning occasionally, until golden brown. Remove from the oil and drain on paper towels or a rack.

Coleslaw

 25 minutes   10 servings

Ingredients

1 medium head of cabbage, cored and shredded

3 carrots, peeled and shredded

½ cup (120 milliliters) parsley, chopped

1 cup (240 milliliters) mayonnaise

2 tablespoons (30 milliliters) apple cider vinegar

2 tablespoons (30 milliliters) dijon mustard

1 teaspoon (5 milliliters) celery seeds

¼ (1.2 milliliters) teaspoon fine sea salt

¼ (1.2 milliliters) teaspoon black pepper

Directions

1. In a large bowl, add cabbage, carrots, and parsley; and toss to mix.
2. In a medium bowl, combine mayonnaise, vinegar, mustard, celery seeds, salt, and pepper.
3. Add the contents of the medium bowl into the large bowl and mix well.

Pork Fried Rice

 18 minutes   3 servings

Ingredients

2 tablespoons (30 milliliters) oyster sauce

1 tablespoon (15 milliliters) light soy sauce

½ tablespoon (7.5 milliliters) dark soy sauce

⅛ teaspoon (0.6 milliliters) ground white pepper

2 tablespoons (30 milliliters) neutral cooking oil, divided

2 eggs, lightly beaten

1 cup (240 milliliters) minced pork

1 small onion, diced

1 tablespoon (15 milliliters) garlic, minced

1 teaspoon (5 milliliters) ginger, minced

½ cup (120 milliliters) peas

½ cup (120 milliliters) carrot, diced

3 cups (720 milliliters) cold cooked white rice

2 scallions, finely chopped for garnishing

TIP
You may replace oyster sauce with vegetarian stir-fry sauce or mushroom vegetarian stir-fry sauce.

Small Plates, Sides & Snacks   **25**

Directions

1. In a small bowl, mix oyster sauce, light soy sauce, dark soy sauce, and white pepper. Set aside.

2. Heat a wok over high heat until smoking hot. Carefully add 1 tablespoon (15 milliliters) of oil, swirling to coat the wok's surface.

3. Pour in the egg. Once it begins to set at the bottom, stir to help the runny part flow. Use a spatula to scramble so that it turns into small pieces. Transfer out and set aside.

4. Pour the remaining 1 tablespoon (15 milliliters) of oil into the wok. Add the minced pork, spreading and flattening it to ensure maximum contact with the wok. Wait for the bottom part to become lightly browned. Then, flip and stir to fry thoroughly.

5. Once the pork loses its pink color, add the onion, garlic, and ginger. Fry until the onion becomes transparent.

6. Stir in the peas and carrots. Fry on high for 30 seconds. Add the rice and egg to the wok. Cook for another 30 to 40 seconds.

7. Pour the sauce mixture over the vegetables. Toss and stir constantly to ensure an even coating. Once all the ingredients are piping hot, turn off the heat. Sprinkle the scallions over the vegetables and give everything a final toss.

Egg Drop Soup

 15 minutes   3 to 4 servings

Ingredients

4 cups (960 milliliters) chicken stock (or vegetable stock)

2 large eggs, lightly beaten

¼ teaspoon (1.2 milliliters) white pepper

¼ teaspoon (1.2 milliliters) salt

1 to 2 spring onions, finely chopped, for garnish

Directions

1. In a wok or saucepan, bring stock to a boil. Very slowly, pour in the eggs in a steady stream.
2. To make shreds, stir the egg quickly in a clockwise direction as you pour for 1 minute. To make thin streams or ribbons, stir the eggs clockwise until they form.
3. Add the pepper, salt, and sesame oil if using. Pour into bowls and garnish with spring onion.

Spring Rolls

 30 minutes   7 servings

Ingredients

2 tablespoons (30 milliliters) vegetable oil

1 clove garlic, minced

2 spring onions, finely chopped

1 carrot, julienned

1 cup (240 milliliters) cabbage, shredded

½ cup (120 milliliters) bean sprouts

7 spring roll wrappers

14 tablespoons (210 milliliters) cooked vermicelli noodles

2 tablespoons (30 milliliters) soy sauce

1 tablespoon (15 milliliters) oyster sauce

1 tablespoon (15 milliliters) sesame oil

1 tablespoon (15 milliliters) sugar

1 tablespoon (15 milliliters) cornstarch mixed with 2 tablespoons (30 milliliters) water (to seal rolls)

½ tablespoon (7.5 milliliters) black pepper

Directions

1. In a large pan over medium-high heat, add 2 tablespoons oil, minced garlic, and chopped spring onions. Sauté until fragrant.
2. Add shredded cabbage, julienned carrots, and bean sprouts. Cook until vegetables are tender-crisp. Stir in cooked vermicelli noodles.

Small Plates, Sides & Snacks

3. Mix soy sauce, oyster sauce, sesame oil, sugar, and pepper in a small bowl. Pour this mixture over the filling mixture and stir well to combine.

4. Once the veggies turn tender, remove the pan from heat and set it aside to cool.

5. Lay a spring roll wrapper on a clean, dry surface, with one corner pointing towards you (diamond shape). Place 2 to 3 tablespoons (30 to 45 milliliters) of filling near the wrapper's bottom corner.

6. Fold the bottom corner over the filling, then tightly roll in the sides. Use the cornstarch mixture to seal the edge of the wrapper. Repeat with the remaining wrappers and filling.

7. Heat the remaining vegetable oil in a deep pan or wok over medium heat.

8. Carefully place spring rolls, seam side down, into the hot oil, a few at a time. Fry until golden brown and crispy, turning occasionally to ensure even cooking.

9. Remove the spring rolls with a slotted spoon and place them on paper towels to drain excess oil.

10. Serve hot with homemade sweet chili, plum, or peanut sauce.

Crab Rangoon

 85 minutes   48 rangoons

Ingredients

1 cup (240 milliliters) block cream cheese, room temperature

1 cup (240 milliliters) fresh or canned crab meat, drained and flaked

1 teaspoon (5 milliliters) red onion, chopped

½ teaspoon (2.5 milliliters) Worcestershire sauce

½ teaspoon (2.5 milliliters) soy sauce

¼ teaspoon (1.2 milliliters) black pepper

1 green onion, finely sliced

1 large clove garlic, smashed, peeled, and finely minced

1 package wonton wrappers or see recipe on page 36

1 small bowl water

oil, for deep frying

DEFINITION
Flake: to break into small pieces using a fork.

Small Plates, Sides & Snacks

Directions

1. In a medium bowl, combine the cream cheese and crab meat.

2. Mix in the red onion, worcestershire, soy sauce, black pepper, green onion, and garlic. Combine thoroughly and set aside.

3. On a flat surface, lay out a wonton wrapper at an angle so it forms a diamond (not a square). Wet the edges of the wrapper by dipping your finger in the water in the bowl and wiping the edges of the wonton.

4. Add 1 teaspoon (5 milliliters) of filling to the middle of the wonton.

5. Carefully bring up the four points of the wrapper so they all meet in the middle but do not touch each other yet. Gently press the sides against the filling, and then adhere all of the edges together so a point forms on top. The dumpling should be a four-sided pyramid with a bottom. Ensure there are no air bubbles by carefully pushing the sides toward each other.

6. Cover the completed crab rangoon with a damp kitchen or paper towel to keep it from drying out while preparing the remainder of the dumplings.

7. Heat a wok or skillet and add enough oil for deep frying.

8. When the oil is ready (the temperature should be 360°F to 375°F (182°C to 190°C), carefully slide in the rangoons, taking care not to overcrowd the wok. Deep-fry until they are golden brown, about 3 minutes, turning once.

9. Remove with a slotted spoon to a paper towel-lined plate and drain. Cook remaining rangoons.

10. Serve hot with sweet and sour sauce or Chinese hot mustard.

Wonton Wrappers

 1 hour

 50 servings

Ingredients

2 cups (480 milliliters) all-purpose flour

1 teaspoon (5 milliliters) salt

1 large egg

½ cup (120 milliliters) cold water, for kneading

½ cup (120 milliliters) flour, for dusting

Directions

1. On a flat surface, mix the flour and salt with clean fingers.
2. Create a well in the center of the flour and add the egg, whisking slowly to incorporate the flour.
3. Add the water a little at a time and work the dough until it holds together and forms a ball.
4. Using your hands, knead the dough for 5-6 minutes. Cover to allow it to rest for 30 minutes.
5. After 30 minutes, knead the dough again for 2 minutes.
6. Roll the dough into a long rope and cut the rope into 50 small pieces. Roll each piece into a 3.5-inch (.08 meter) square.
7. To keep the wonton wrappers from sticking together, dust each with flour and stack them in a pile; now the wrappers are ready to be filled.

Steamed Vegetable Dumplings

 40 minutes   20 dumplings

Ingredients

1 tablespoon (15 milliliters) sesame oil

1 cup (240 milliliters) shimeji mushrooms

¼ cup (60 milliliters) purple cabbage, shredded

¼ cup (60 milliliters) brown or white rice

1 large carrot, peeled and diced

½ cup (120 milliliters) spinach

1 tablespoon (15 milliliters) miso paste

1 tablespoon (15 milliliters) sushi ginger, raw

20 dumpling wrappers or Wonton Wrappers, see recipe on page 36

Tamari for dipping

Furikake for dipping

TIP
Oyster, straw, or button mushrooms can replace shimeji mushrooms.

Small Plates, Sides & Snacks   37

Directions

1. In a large skillet or wok, heat sesame oil over medium heat. After about 30 seconds, add the shimeji mushrooms, purple cabbage, rice, and diced carrots. Stir every minute or so for 8 to 10 minutes or until slightly tender. Add in the spinach and cook no more than a minute. Remove from heat and allow to cool.

2. While the veggies are cooling, prepare dumpling station – start heating water in your frying pan with a bamboo steamer rack on top. Lay out your dumpling wrappers on a cutting board. Fill a small dish with water.

3. Once your veggies have cooled down, add them to a food processor along with the miso paste and ginger. Pulse a few times, making sure not to over blend – mixture should be rough. Add mixture to a mixing bowl.

4. Use your finger to add a thin layer of water to the edges of your dumpling wrapper. Fill the dumpling wrapper with a small amount of the mixture. Fold the mixture in half and press the wrapper edges together to stick. Make sure to press the filling inwards to avoid spillage.

5. The water should be lightly boiling in your frying pan. Add parchment paper to your bamboo steamer rack to prevent the dumplings from getting stuck to the tray; arrange them on your steamer rack. Make sure they're not too crowded before closing the lid.

6. Let the dumplings steam for about 12 to 15 minutes. Use chopsticks to gently remove them from your tray. Repeat until you have used all of the filling and wrappers.

7. Enjoy with soy sauce.

Small Plates, Sides & Snacks

Tomato and Egg Noodle Soup

 15 minutes   2 servings

Ingredients

3 eggs

1 tablespoon (15 milliliters) water

2½ tablespoons (37.5 milliliters) canola oil, divided

2 cloves garlic, minced

4 tomatoes, diced

1 ½ cups (360 milliliters) water

¾ teaspoon (3.6 milliliters) salt

¼ teaspoon (1.2 milliliters) sugar

2 portions noodles, homemade (see recipe on page 48) or store-bought

1 stalk scallions, finely chopped

Directions

1. In a medium bowl, beat the eggs with the water until a little foamy.
2. In a skillet or wok, heat 2 tablespoons (30 milliliters) of oil until hot. Pour in the eggs. Push eggs with a spatula to cook evenly and break the eggs into pieces. Dish out as soon as no runny part is left.
3. Add the remaining ½ tablespoon (7.5 milliliters) of oil to the wok. Fry garlic until fragrant, then add tomatoes. Cook until the tomatoes appear mushy on the edge.
4. Pour in 1 ½ cups (360 milliliters) of water. Bring to a boil then leave to simmer for 2 minutes. Add salt, sugar and the cooked egg. Stir well to combine.
5. Boil the noodles of your choice until fully cooked (don't overcook though). Rinse briefly under running water, then drain well.
6. Put the noodles into serving bowls. Add the tomato and egg soup. Garnish with chopped scallions. Serve immediately.

Small Plates, Sides & Snacks

Broccoli with Garlic Sauce

 7 minutes   4 Servings

Ingredients

2 tablespoons (30 milliliters) vegetable oil

2 garlic cloves, minced

1 teaspoon (5 milliliters) fresh minced ginger

2 tablespoons (30 milliliters) water

1 ½ tablespoons (22.5 milliliters) miso paste

1 tablespoon (15 milliliters) soy sauce

1 teaspoon (5 milliliters) sesame oil

1 pound (454 grams) broccoli, trimmed into bite-sized florets and steamed

Directions

1. Heat a large non-stick skillet over medium heat, then add the vegetable oil; when hot, add the garlic and ginger, stirring constantly until fragrant, about 15 seconds.
2. In a small bowl, stir the water, miso paste, soy sauce, and sesame oil, then pour into the skillet. Stir constantly for an additional 15 seconds, until slightly thickened.
3. Add the steamed broccoli, being careful not to pour any water from the bowl into the skillet. Toss to coat.

TIP

The easiest way to steam broccoli is to place it in a microwave-safe bowl with 3 tablespoons (45 milliliters) of water. Top with a microwave-safe plate and microwave on high for 3 minutes.

Small Plates, Sides & Snacks

Entrées

Chicken Stir Fry 46
Easy Homemade Noodles 48
Birthday Noodles with Peanut Sauce 50
Sweet and Sour Chicken 52
Beef Lo Mein 54
Sesame Chicken 56
Vegetable Stir Fry 58
Chicken Chow Mein 60
Sweet and Sour Spareribs 62
Sesame Noodles 64

Chicken Stir Fry

 40 minutes   6 servings

Ingredients

⅓ cup (80 milliliters) cornstarch

1 pound (454 grams) boneless chicken breasts, diced

1 tablespoon (15 milliliters) ginger, minced

1 tablespoon (15 milliliters) garlic, minced

¼ cup (60 milliliters) soy sauce

½ cup (120 milliliters) orange marmalade

¼ tablespoon (3.75 milliliters) red pepper flakes

¼ teaspoon (1.2 milliliters) kosher salt

¼ teaspoon black pepper (1.2 milliliters)

2 tablespoons (30 milliliters) canola oil

1 red pepper, thinly sliced

1 green pepper, thinly sliced

Directions

1. Add cornstarch to a sealed bag, add chicken cubes, and toss to coat well.
2. In a small bowl, whisk ginger, garlic, soy sauce, marmalade, and red pepper flakes. Season with salt and pepper.
3. Heat a skillet or wok and add canola oil.
4. Fry the chicken on medium heat until the chicken turns golden brown add peppers and cook until soft.
5. Add the sauce and stir-fry to coat the chicken.

Entrées

Easy Homemade Noodles

 45 minutes   4 servings

Ingredients

1 ½ cups (360 milliliters) all-purpose flour, plus extra for dusting
¼ teaspoons (1.2 milliliters) salt
⅔ cup (160 milliliters) water
1 tablespoon (15 milliliters) cornmeal

Directions

1. In a large bowl, mix flour and salt. Gradually add water while stirring constantly to distribute the liquid evenly.
2. Combine with your clean hands into a rough-looking dough. Cover, then leave to rest for 30 minutes.
3. Knead the dough for about 3 minutes until it becomes very smooth.
4. With a rolling pin, gradually flatten the dough into a sheet about 0.79 inches (2 millimeters) thick. During this process, flip and turn the dough as often as necessary to achieve an even thickness. Remember to dust the surface and the dough with flour to prevent sticking.
5. Once the dough is rolled to your desired thickness, spread cornmeal over and underneath. Then, fold the dough sheet into a band of 4 to 5 layers. Use a sharp, dry knife to cut it into thin strips.
6. Gently unfold and loosen the noodles with your hands.
7. Bring a large pot of water to a full boil. Add the noodles and cook over high heat. Once the water boils again, pour in ½ cup (120 milliliters) cold water.
8. Cook the noodles for a further 1 to 2 minutes (the time required depends on the size of your noodles).
9. Rinse the noodles under cold water to remove excess starch and drain well. Serve in soup or with sauce and toppings.

Birthday Noodles with Peanut Sauce

 30 minutes   4 servings

Ingredients

2 tablespoons (30 milliliters) smooth peanut butter or sesame paste

¼ cup (60 milliliters) hot water

3 tablespoons (45 milliliters) soy sauce

1 teaspoon (5 milliliters) honey

4 cups (960 milliliters) cooked Chinese-style noodles (see recipe on page 48) or spaghetti

2 scallions, cut in ½ inch (1.25-centimeter) pieces

Bean sprouts, optional

Chopped peanuts, optional

Directions

1. In a large bowl, use a fork to stir the peanut butter or sesame paste with the water until it is creamy. Stir in the soy sauce and honey; set aside.
2. Drain the cooked noodles, add the peanut butter mixture to the bowl, and toss well.
3. Serve the noodles cold, topped with scallions, sprouts, or chopped peanuts.

Sweet and Sour Chicken

 25 minutes   4 servings

Ingredients

4 tablespoons (60 milliliters) vegetable oil

1 carrot, peeled and sliced

1 red pepper, sliced

1 onion, thinly sliced

1 clove garlic, crushed

½ teaspoon (2 centimeters) fresh ginger root, grated

2 tablespoons (30 milliliters) dark brown sugar

1 tablespoon (15 milliliters) tomato purée

¼ cup (60 milliliters) vinegar

1 tablespoon (15 milliliters) dark soy sauce

2 cups (480 milliliters) chicken stock

1 tablespoon (15 milliliters) plain flour

¼ (1.2 milliliters) teaspoon salt

¼ (1.2 milliliters) teaspoon pepper

2 cups (480 milliliters) chicken breast, diced

2 cups (480 milliliters) pineapple, chopped (reserve juice)

Spring onions, chopped to garnish

Directions

1. In a large skillet, heat oil, add carrot and pepper, then sauté with grated ginger and crushed garlic.
2. Add the pineapple juice, tomato purée, sugar, vinegar, soy sauce, and chicken stock; stir well.
3. Season with salt and pepper.
4. Add the chicken pieces after tossing them in the flour.
5. Then, cover the skillet and cook until the chicken and vegetables are tender.
6. Add the pineapple chunks and stir. Garnish with spring onions and serve hot.

Beef Lo Mein

 40 minutes   4 Servings

Ingredients

1-pound (454 grams) boneless beef top sirloin steak, sliced lengthwise and then crosswise into thin slices

4 cloves garlic, minced

2 teaspoons (10 milliliters) fresh ginger, minced

¾ teaspoon (3.6 milliliters) red pepper flakes, divided

1 tablespoon (15 milliliters) vegetable oil

1 14-ounce (400 grams) can of vegetable broth

1 cup (240 milliliters) water

2 tablespoons (30 milliliters) soy sauce

1 8-ounce (224 grams) package frozen mixed vegetables for stir-fry or fresh vegetables of your choice

1 9-ounce (250 grams) package refrigerated angel hair pasta or 8 ounces (224 grams) dried angel hair pasta

¼ cup (60 milliliters) chopped fresh cilantro, optional for garnish

Directions

1. In a medium bowl, combine beef, garlic, ginger, and ½ teaspoon (2.5 milliliters) red pepper flakes; and mix well.

2. Heat oil in a skillet or wok over medium-high heat. Add half of the beef; stir-fry for 2 minutes or until the meat is barely pink in the center. Remove to a plate. Repeat with remaining beef.

3. Add broth, water, soy sauce, and remaining ½ teaspoon (2.5 milliliters) red pepper flakes to wok; boil over high heat. Add vegetables; return to a boil. Reduce heat to low; cover and simmer for 3 minutes or until vegetables are crisp-tender.

4. Stir in pasta; return to a boil over high heat. Reduce heat to medium; cook, uncovered, 2 minutes, separating pasta with two forks. Return beef and any accumulated juices to pan; cook 1 minute or until pasta is tender and beef is heated. Sprinkle with cilantro, if desired.

Sesame Chicken

 40 minutes   6 servings

Ingredients

For the chicken

1 ½ lbs boneless skinless chicken breasts cut into 1-inch pieces
2 eggs beaten
¼ teaspoon salt
¼ teaspoon pepper
½ cup all-purpose flour
½ cup cornstarch
Oil for frying

For the sauce

1 teaspoon vegetable oil
1 teaspoon minced fresh garlic
¼ cup honey
¼ cup soy sauce
2 tablespoons ketchup
3 tablespoons brown sugar
2 tablespoons rice vinegar
1 tablespoon toasted sesame oil
2 teaspoons cornstarch
2 tablespoons sesame seeds
2 tablespoons sliced green onions

Directions

1. Place the eggs, salt, and pepper in a bowl. Stir to combine.
2. Place the flour and ½ cup of cornstarch in a shallow bowl or plate. Stir to combine.
3. Dip each piece of chicken into the egg mixture, then into the flour. Repeat the process with all of the chicken.
4. Heat oil in a deep pan to 350°F.
5. Add 7-8 pieces of chicken to the pan. Cook for 5 minutes or until crispy and golden brown. Repeat the process with the remaining chicken. Drain the chicken on paper towels.
6. In a small bowl, combine the honey, soy sauce, ketchup, brown sugar, rice vinegar, sesame oil, and cornstarch.
7. Heat the oil in a large pan over medium heat. Add the garlic and cook for 30 seconds. Add the honey sauce mixture and bring to a simmer. Cook for 3-4 minutes or until just thickened.
8. Add the crispy chicken to the pan and toss to coat with the sauce. Sprinkle with sesame seeds and green onions, then serve.

Vegetable Stir Fry

 25 minutes   4 servings

Ingredients

1 large carrot, sliced
2 cups (480 milliliters) medium broccoli florets
1 cup (240 milliliters) can baby corn spears, drained
1 cup (240 milliliters) mushrooms (white or brown), sliced or quartered
1 whole pepper (red, yellow or orange), seeded and sliced
2 tablespoons (30 milliliters) cooking oil (extra light olive oil or canola)
2 tablespoons (30 milliliters) unsalted butter
3 garlic cloves, peeled and minced
2 teaspoons (10 milliliters) ginger, minced
¼ cup (60 milliliters) vegetable broth
½ tsp (2.5 milliliters) cornstarch
3 tablespoons (45 milliliters) soy sauce
2 tablespoons (30 milliliters) honey
¼ teaspoon (1.2 milliliters) hot sauce, optional

Directions

1. Heat the oil in a large non-stick skillet or wok over medium heat. Add the carrot, broccoli, corn, mushrooms, and pepper, and stir fry for about 3 minutes or until crisp-tender. Add the butter, garlic, and ginger and cook until fragrant.
2. In a small bowl, combine broth, cornstarch, soy sauce, honey, and hot sauce (if using) for the stir-fry sauce. Pour the sauce over the vegetables and stir.
3. Turn the heat down to medium-low and cook for 3 to 4 minutes, until the sauce thickens and the vegetables are the desired tenderness.

Chicken Chow Mein

 15 minutes   2 servings

Ingredients

1 6.3-ounce (180 grams) chicken breast, thinly sliced

½ tablespoon (7.5 milliliters) cornstarch

¼ teaspoon (1.2 milliliters) salt

1 tablespoon (15 milliliters) water

1 teaspoon (5 milliliters) sesame oil

1 tablespoon (15 milliliters) light soy sauce

1 teaspoon (5 milliliters) dark soy sauce

1 tablespoon (15 milliliters) oyster sauce

1 pinch freshly-ground black pepper

2 tablespoons (30 milliliters) vegetable oil, divided

1 stalk scallions, chopped, white and green parts divided

2 cloves garlic, sliced

Fresh chili, sliced to taste

1 head bok choy, sliced

1½ cups (360 milliliters) bean sprouts

14 ounces (400 grams) ready-to-fry chow mein noodles/Chinese egg noodles

Directions

1. In a large bowl, add chicken (or alternative), cornstarch, salt, and water; and mix until combined.
2. Pour in sesame oil and stir to coat evenly.
3. In a medium bowl, mix light soy sauce, dark soy sauce, oyster sauce, and black pepper. Set aside.
4. Heat a skillet or wok until very hot. Add 1 tablespoon (15 milliliters) of oil. Stir in the chicken slices. Fry until they lose their pinkness and turn pale (do not overcook); transfer to a plate.
5. Pour the remaining 1 tablespoon (15 milliliters) of oil into the wok. Sauté garlic, fresh chili, and the white part of the scallion until fragrant. Add noodles and stir fry for 1 minute.
6. Add the chicken, bok choy, and bean sprouts, then pour in the sauce mixture. Toss and mix until the seasoning is evenly distributed and everything becomes piping hot.
7. Garnish with the green part of the scallion. Place onto plates and serve immediately. If you wish, drizzle some homemade chili oil over the top.

60   Entrées

TIP
Great alternatives for chicken are eggs (for vegetarians) and tofu (for vegan diets). Replace bok choy with crunchy vegetables of your choice - celery, cabbage, carrot, snow peas, baby corn, or bell peppers.

Sweet and Sour Spareribs

 1 hour 12 minutes

 3 servings

Ingredients

2 cups water
1 ½ pounds (681 grams) pork ribs
1 tablespoon (15 milliliters) olive oil
10 cloves garlic, whole
1 thumb-sized piece fresh ginger
2 stalks scallions, cut into halves
5 tablespoons (75 milliliters) white sugar
4 tablespoons (60 milliliters) black rice vinegar, divided
1 tablespoon (15 milliliters) light soy sauce
1 teaspoon (5 milliliters) dark soy sauce
⅛ teaspoon (0.6 milliliters) salt
Toasted sesame seeds for garnish
Scallions, finely chopped for garnish

Directions

1. Fill a pot with water, add spareribs, bring to a boil, and then reduce to a simmer.
2. Skim off the foam forming on the water with a large spoon. After about 3 minutes, drain the ribs.
3. Pour oil into a deep pan or wok; and add the drained ribs, garlic, ginger, and scallion. Stir fry over medium heat until the ribs become golden on the surface.
4. Add sugar, black rice vinegar (keep 1 tablespoon (15 milliliters) for later use), light soy sauce, dark soy sauce, and salt. Top up with hot water enough to just level with the ribs.
5. Bring to a full boil, then turn the heat to low. Cover and leave to simmer for about 50 minutes.
6. Uncover and pick out all the garlic, ginger, and scallions when the time is up. Add the remaining 1 tablespoon (15 milliliters) of black rice vinegar. Turn the heat to high to boil down the liquid.
7. Stir from time to time once the liquid becomes just thick enough to coat the ribs. Remove from the heat immediately. Be attentive not to overcook (approx. 8 min).
8. Transfer the ribs to a serving bowl/plate. Sprinkle sesame seeds and scallions on top to garnish.

62 Entrées

Sesame Noodles

 10 minutes   2 servings

Ingredients

¼ cup (60 milliliters) Chinese sesame paste
2 tablespoons (30 milliliters) light soy sauce
2 tablespoons (30 milliliters) Chinese black vinegar
1 tablespoon (15 milliliters) sugar
1 tablespoon (15 milliliters) chili oil
1 tablespoon (15 milliliters) water
3 cloves garlic, grated
1 cup (240 milliliters) dried noodles
½ cup (120 milliliters) reserved noodle cooking water
2 scallions, chopped for garnish
1 cucumber, thinly sliced for garnish
Peanuts, crushed for garnish

TIP
Transfer the noodles directly to the sauce if you want to enjoy this dish hot. If eating the dish cold, rinse the noodles under cold water and drain well.

Directions

1. In a medium bowl, mix sesame paste, soy sauce, vinegar, sugar, chili oil, water and garlic. Whisk until combined and the sauce is smooth.
2. Cook noodles according to package directions (or see homemade noodle recipe on page 46), reserving about ½ cup (120 milliliters) of noodle-cooking water.
3. Once the noodles are mixed with the sauce, use the reserved noodle cooking water to thin the sauce as needed. Garnish with scallions, sliced cucumber, and crushed peanuts.

Desserts

Fortune Cookies 68
Snowflake Cake 71
Nian Gao (Lunar New Year Cake)..74
Chocolate Soymilk Pudding 76
Almond Cookies 78
Fried Ice Cream 80
Salted Butterscotch Sauce 82
Hong Kong Egg Tarts 83
Butter Pastry Tart Crust 85

Fortune Cookies

 30 minutes   10 servings

Ingredients

2 large egg whites

½ teaspoon (2.5 milliliters) pure vanilla extract

½ teaspoon (2.5 milliliters) almond extract

3 tablespoons (45 milliliters) vegetable oil

½ cup (120 milliliters) all-purpose flour

1 ½ teaspoons (7.5 milliliters) cornstarch

¼ teaspoon (1.2 milliliters) salt

½ cup (120 milliliters) sugar

3 teaspoons (15 milliliters) water

Directions

1. To create fortunes, cut pieces pieces of paper into 3 ½ inch (8.75 centimeter) long and ½ inch (1.25 centimeter) wide pieces. Be creative and write fortunes on the slips of paper.
2. Preheat oven to 300°F (150°C) and grease two 9 x 13 inch (23 x 33 centimeter) baking sheets.
3. In a medium bowl, lightly beat the egg whites, vanilla extract, almond extract, and vegetable oil until frothy but not stiff.
4. In a separate bowl, sift the flour, cornstarch, salt, and sugar. Stir in the water and mix to combine.

Desserts

5. Add the flour mixture to the egg-white mixture and stir until you have a smooth batter. The batter should not be runny but drop quickly off a wooden spoon.

6. Place level tablespoons of batter onto the cookie sheet, spacing them at least 3 inches (7.5 centimeters) apart. Tilt the baking sheet back and forth and from side to side so that each tablespoon of batter forms a circle 4 inches (10 centimeter) in diameter.

7. Bake until the outer ½ inch (1.25 centimeters) of each cookie turns golden brown and is easy to remove from the baking sheet with a spatula (14 to 15 minutes).

8. Working quickly, remove the cookie with a spatula and flip it over in your hand.

9. Place a fortune in the middle of a cookie.

10. To form the fortune cookie shape, fold the cookie in half, then gently pull the edges downward over the rim of a glass, wooden spoon, or muffin tin's edge. Place the finished cookie in the cup of the muffin tin so that it keeps its shape. Continue with the rest of the cookies.

Snowflake Cake

 2 hours and 25 minutes   10 servings

Ingredients

Strawberry Snowflake Cake

¼ cup (60 milliliters) strawberries

2 cups (480 milliliters) water

14 tablespoons (210 milliliters) superfine sugar

5 leaves gelatin

1 cup (240 milliliters) whole milk

¼ cup (60 milliliters) heavy cream, or whipping cream

9 tablespoons (135 milliliters) potato starch, or corn flour

7 tablespoons (105 milliliters) water

3 tablespoons (45 milliliters) shredded coconut

Coconut Snowflake Cake

1 cup (240 milliliters) coconut

2 cups (480 milliliters) water

14 tablespoons (210 milliliters) superfine sugar

¼ cup (60 milliliters) heavy cream, or whipping cream

5 leaves gelatin

9 tablespoons (135 milliliters) potato starch, or corn flour

7 tablespoons (105 milliliters) water

3 tablespoons (45 milliliters) shredded coconut

> **TIP**
> You can make two cakes or stack them to make one double layered cake.

Desserts   **71**

Directions

Strawberry Snowflake Cake

1. In a small saucepan, add 1½ cups (355 milliliters) of water, strawberries, and superfine sugar and bring to a boil. Keep whisking it while cooking to help the sugar and strawberries dissolve.

2. Soften gelatin in cold water.

3. Add milk and heavy cream to the cooked strawberry jam and bring it to a boil again. After it has boiled, turn off the stove and leave it for 10 minutes.

4. Add gelatin and keep whisking it to help it mix evenly.

5. Mix starch and the additional ½ cup (118 milliliters) of water evenly and add it to the strawberry-gelatin mixture.

6. Line a baking pan with parchment paper. Pour the mixture into this pan and leave it in a fridge for a couple of hours to help it form.

7. Slice the snowflake cakes and coat them with shredded coconut, and they're ready to serve.

Coconut Snowflake Cake

1. In a medium saucepan, add coconut milk, water, superfine sugar, and heavy cream; use a whisk to mix and bring to a boil, then simmer for 5 to 10 minutes. Remove from heat and leave it for 10 minutes to cool down.

2. Soften gelatin in cold water and stir it into the cool coconut mixture.

3. Add starch to the coconut-gelatin mixture.

4. Line a baking pan with parchment paper. Pour the mixture into this pan and leave it in the fridge for a couple of hours to help it form.

5. Slice the snowflake cakes and coat them with shredded coconut; they're ready to serve.

Nian Gao (Lunar New Year Cake)

 60 Minutes   8 to 10 servings

Ingredients

2 cups (480 milliliters) mochiko sweet rice flour, plus a bit extra for sprinkling on the baking dish

¾ cup (175 milliliters) vegetable oil

3 large eggs

2 ½ cups (600 milliliters) milk

1 cup (240 milliliters) sugar

1 tablespoon (15 milliliters) baking soda

1 15-ounce (425 grams) can red azuki beans

TIP
A replacement for mochiko sweet rice flour is glutinous rice flour or cornstarch. Do not use enriched white flour.

Directions

1. Preheat the oven to 350°F (180°C). Grease a 9 x 13-inch (23 x 33-centimeter) baking pan with nonstick cooking spray.
2. In a large bowl, add sweet rice flour, oil, eggs, milk, sugar, and baking soda and mix until well combined.
3. Sprinkle the extra mochiko flour into the baking dish, then add half of the batter.
4. Spread the red adzuki beans on top. (If the beans are too thick to spread, mix some batter into them.)
5. Spread the other half of the batter over the red azuki beans. Bake for 40 to 50 minutes. Test for doneness by inserting a toothpick in the middle; if it comes out clean, it's done.

74   Desserts

Chocolate Soymilk Pudding

 1 hour 5 minutes   10 servings

Ingredients

2 cups (480 milliliters) soymilk

½ cup (120 milliliters) sugar

¼ cup (60 milliliters) cocoa powder

¼ cup (60 milliliters) gelatin

Whipped cream

Chocolate shavings

Directions

1. In a medium saucepan over medium heat, combine the soy milk, sugar, cocoa powder, and gelatin. Bring the mixture to a boil, stirring constantly.
2. Reduce the heat and let the mixture simmer for 5 minutes, continuing to stir.
3. Remove the saucepan from the heat and pour the mixture into individual serving glasses or molds.
4. Allow the pudding to cool completely at room temperature, then refrigerate for at least 2 hours to set.
5. Before serving, garnish with whipped cream and chocolate shavings.

Almond Cookies

 30 minutes   24 cookies

Ingredients

1 cup (240 milliliters) unsalted butter, softened

1 cup (240 milliliters) granulated sugar

1 tablespoon (15 milliliters) almond extract

½ tablespoon (7.5 milliliters) vanilla extract

2 cups (480 milliliters) all-purpose flour

½ tablespoon (7.5 milliliters) baking powder

½ cup (120 milliliters) almond flour (or finely ground almonds)

¼ tablespoon (3.75 milliliters) salt

1 egg, beaten (for egg wash)

Whole almonds for garnish, optional

Directions

1. Preheat your oven to 325°F (165°C) and line baking sheets with parchment paper.
2. In a medium bowl, mix the butter and granulated sugar using a hand mixer until it turns into a light and fluffy mixture.
3. Add almond and vanilla extracts. Mix well until everything is thoroughly combined.
4. In another medium bowl, whisk together the flour, baking powder, almond flour, and salt.
5. Gradually add the dry ingredients to the sugar-butter mixture, mixing until a soft dough forms. It should be slightly sticky but manageable. Take tablespoon-sized portions of dough and roll them into balls. Place the balls on the prepared baking sheets, spacing them about 2 inches (5 centimeters) apart.
6. Flatten each ball slightly with the palm of your hand, and gently press a whole almond into the center of each cookie.
7. Brush the tops of the cookies with beaten egg, which will give them a nice shine after baking.
8. Put the cookies into the oven and bake for 12 to 15 minutes until they turn light golden.
9. Transfer the cookies to a wire rack and allow to cool.

Fried Ice Cream

 2 hours 15 minutes   4 servings

Ingredients

2 cups (480 milliliters) full-fat vanilla ice cream

1 egg

2 tablespoons (30 milliliters) milk

1 cup (240 milliliters) fine dry breadcrumbs

Vegetable oil, for deep-frying

Directions

1. Roll ice cream into 4 balls, place on a parchment paper-lined plate, and return to freezer until very hard.
2. In a shallow bowl, lightly beat egg and milk together.
3. In a second shallow bowl, add breadcrumbs.
4. Working one at a time, dip balls into egg mixture, then roll in breadcrumbs, pressing them on firmly. Return to the plate and freeze until stiff.
5. Repeat the egg and breadcrumb mixture twice, pressing and rolling the balls in your hands to coat them firmly and give them a smooth shape, returning them to the freezer for at least an hour between coatings.
6. Return to freezer until very hard, preferably overnight.
7. Heat oil in a saucepan until very hot.
8. One at a time, use a slotted spoon to lower the balls into the oil for 20 to 30 seconds, just until they're golden brown. Drain on a paper towel.
9. Serve deep-fried ice cream immediately with Salted Butterscotch Sauce.

Salted Butterscotch Sauce

 10 minutes   10 servings

Ingredients

4 tablespoons (60 milliliters) unsalted butter

½ cup (120 milliliters) brown sugar

½ cup (120 milliliters) heavy cream

1 teaspoon (5 milliliters) salt

1 teaspoon (5 milliliters) vanilla extract

Directions

1. In a saucepan, combine butter, sugar, cream, and salt and boil, stirring occasionally. Remove from heat, stir in vanilla and let cool.

Hong Kong Egg Tarts

 55 minutes   12 tarts

Ingredients

½ cup (120 milliliters) warm water or warm milk

¼ cup (60 milliliters) evaporated whole milk

¼ cup (60 milliliters) sugar

2 large eggs

2 large egg yolks

1 teaspoon (5 milliliters) pure vanilla extract

¼ teaspoon (1.2 milliliters) sea salt

1 package frozen egg tart crust (or see recipe on page 85)

Directions

1. Preheat oven to 395°F (190°C).
2. Remove frozen tart shells from the freezer to allow them to defrost slightly while making the custard filling.
3. In a large bowl, combine warm water, evaporated whole milk, sugar, eggs, egg yolks, vanilla, and salt.
4. Using a fork, slowly combine the ingredients.
5. Strain the egg mixture through a sieve into a pourable container to remove any egg solids and eliminate the air bubbles.
6. Pour the egg mixture into each tart shell until 80% filled, as the egg mixture will expand in the oven.
7. Bake for 15 to 18 minutes until the crusts are golden brown and the egg custard is set. Do not overbake.

Butter Pastry Tart Crust

 35 minutes   8 servings

Ingredients

1 ½ cups (360 milliliters) all-purpose flour, sifted

⅛ teaspoon (0.6 milliliters) salt

½ cup (120 milliliters) butter

1 egg yolk

3 tablespoons (45 milliliters) cold water

Directions

1. Preheat oven to 350° F (190°C).
2. In a medium bowl, cut the butter into the flour and salt, then mix with the egg yolk. Gradually add the water and shape it into a ball. Roll out the dough and fit it into tart pans.
3. Bake for 12 to 14 minutes, until golden around the edges.
4. Let the tarts cool before filling.

TIP
You will need small mini aluminum foil disposable baking tart pans - 3⅜-inch (8.6-centimeter) pie tins.

Desserts

The Great Wall of China

The Great Wall is one of the seven construction wonders in the world not only for its long history, but also for its massive size and its unique architectural style. The Great Wall is the longest man-made structure in the world. It is a series of walls winding up and down across steep mountains and plateaus, totaling about 13,000 miles (21,000 kilometers) in length. It includes beacon towers, barracks, and fortresses along the walls. The average height of the Great Wall is 25.7 feet (7.8 meters), but it reaches about 46 feet (14 meters) in some sections. It would take about 18 months to walk the entire length.

Emperor Qin Shi Huang ordered the construction of the Great Wall around 221 B.C., and it took over 2,000 years to construct (7th century BC – 17th century AD). The wall was built to protect the Chinese Empire from foreign invaders, create a barrier between northern and southern civilizations, and protect the Silk Road trade. The Silk Road, the ancient trade route linking China with the West, transported goods between Rome and China. Silk went westward, while wool, gold, and silver went east.

In ancient times, without electricity and machinery, the only way to transport vast numbers of bricks, lime, and stones to a construction site on a mountain involved either animals or people carrying the materials on their backs and shoulders. Over time, the Great Wall used around 100,000,000 tons of stone, bricks, and mud. Military soldiers, civilian men, and prisoners were the primary sources of manpower. It is said that as many as 400,000 people died building the Great Wall. Legend has it that many of these workers were buried within the wall, but this remains unproven.

Who knew? Workers combined sweet rice flour and slaked lime during the Ming dynasty to create the first composite mortar in history. Portions of the wall built using this "rice mortar" still stand today.

Unfortunately, most Great Wall sections built before the Ming Dynasty (1368–1644) have almost disappeared, so the Chinese government has put regulations into effect to protect the Wall. Stealing rocks, graffiti, and littering are all condemned. Vegetation and trees have been planted in rural areas to decrease erosion and harm caused by storms and other natural disasters. Many popular Great Wall sections, such as Badaling, Mutianyu, and Juyongguan, have been restored and protected.

Ironically, the Great Wall was built to keep foreigners out, but today, the Wall is China's top tourist site, attracting over 4 million domestic and international tourists each year to appreciate its historical and architectural magnificence, as well as the stunning scenery seen from the Wall.

Chinese New Year

Chinese New Year is a 15-day celebration tied to the lunar calendar. It typically begins with the first new moon at the end of January and spans the first 15 days of the first month of the lunar calendar until the full moon arrives.

Houses are thoroughly cleaned in preparation for the Lunar New Year, which signifies the removal of the old and the welcoming of the new. Cleaning is also meant to open space for goodwill and good luck.

Each year, the lunar calendar is represented by one of the 12 zodiac animals. These animals are part of a cycle of 12 stations or "signs" along the sun's path through the cosmos.

The 12 zodiac animals are the rat, ox, tiger, rabbit, dragon, snake, horse, sheep, monkey, rooster, dog, and pig. Which animal is your favorite? In addition to the animals, the five elements of earth, water, fire, wood, and metal are also mapped onto the traditional lunar calendar. Each year is associated with an animal that corresponds to an element.

In Chinese traditions, food is pivotal in fostering connections and expressing respect. The New Year's Eve dinner is the most important meal for Chinese families. Most families gather at a family member's home instead of a restaurant to eat this meal.

Foods made from glutinous rice are commonly eaten, representing togetherness; dumplings, representing wealth; fish for abundance; and crisp golden spring rolls symbolize bars of gold to bring wealth and prosperity in the coming year.

The Color Red
The color red denotes good luck/fortune and happiness/abundance and is often worn or used for decoration in celebrations.

Hongbao (Red Envelopes)
Families unite, exchanging red envelopes filled with money to signify blessings and generosity for a prosperous year ahead. Elders give hongbao to children during the New Year Festival. It is believed that the money and red envelopes will keep evil from the children, keep them healthy, and give them a long life.

Fireworks and Firecrackers
These are used to scare away evil spirits and monsters.

Dragons
The dragon is present in many Chinese cultural celebrations, as the Chinese people often think of themselves as descendants of the mythical creature. On the fifth day of the New Year, when many people must start returning to work, there are numerous dancing dragon performances. The dragon represents prosperity, good luck, and good fortune.

Lantern Festival
The holiday concludes with the Lantern Festival, celebrated on the last day of the New Year's festivities. Parades, dances, games, and fireworks mark the finale. This festival marks the end of the Chinese New Year and the first full moon of the new lunar year. It's a time to promote peace, reconciliation, and forgiveness.

Culinary Passport

Document your journey around the globe with the fun and interactive

- Make it your own by filling in your personal details.
- Packed with useful cooking tips and terms.
- Space for journal notes and celebration stickers.

Culinary Passport included when you buy the *Global Cookbook, Delicious Recipes from Seven Continents.*

ISBN: 978-1-943016-22-8

Download a free culinary passport pdf. This passport has all pages; it does not contain the stickers found in the culinary passport sold with the *Global Cookbook, Delicious Recipes from Seven Continents.*

www.kitcheninkpublishing.com

Culinary Passport Series

Discover recipes from all over the world!

Travel around the world from your kitchen.

Where do you want to travel next?